CHRISTIAN CHARACTER

12 STUDIES FOR INDIVIDUALS OR GROUPS

Andrea Sterk &
Peter Scazzero

With Notes for Leaders

An imprint of InterVarsity Press
Downers Grove, Illinois

InterVarsity Press
P.O. Box 1400, Downers Grove, IL 60515
World Wide Web: www.ivpress.com
E-mail: mail@ivpress.com

©1985, 1999 by InterVarsity Christian Fellowship of the United States of America

All rights reserved. No part of this book may be reproduced in any form without written permission from InterVarsity Press.

InterVarsity Press® is the book-publishing division of InterVarsity Christian Fellowship/USA®, a student movement active on campus at hundreds of universities, colleges and schools of nursing in the United States of America, and a member movement of the International Fellowship of Evangelical Students. For information about local and regional activities, write Public Relations Dept., InterVarsity Christian Fellowship/USA, 6400 Schroeder Rd., P.O. Box 7895, Madison, WI 53707-7895, or visit the IVCF website at <www.intervarsity.org>.

LifeGuide® is a registered trademark of InterVarsity Christian Fellowship.

All Scripture quotations, unless otherwise indicated, are taken from the Holy Bible, New International Version®. NIV®. *Copyright ©1973, 1978, 1984 by International Bible Society. Used by permission of Zondervan Publishing House. All rights reserved.*

Cover photograph: Dennis Flaherty

ISBN-10: 0-8308-3054-5
ISBN-13: 978-0-8308-3054-1

Printed in the United States of America ♾

P 26 25 24 23 22 21 20 19 18 17
Y 22 21 20 19 18 17 16 15

Contents

Getting the Most Out of *Christian Character*

Justin Martyr, Augustine of Hippo, John Wycliffe, Martin Luther, John Calvin, Jonathan Edwards, John Wesley, George Whitefield, Martin Luther King Jr., Billy Graham, Mother Teresa. All of these people were anointed by God in an extraordinary way and endowed with "spectacular" gifts which caused them to stand out from rank-and-file Christians. They were, and continue to be, greatly used to advance the kingdom of God.

At the same time there have been millions throughout the world who have lived godly lives and yet have died in virtual obscurity. The Moravian Christians are a striking example. By their deep piety and good works, they profoundly influenced John Wesley prior to his conversion. Traveling from England to the United States in 1736, Wesley recorded his impressions of these Moravians in his journal:

> At seven I went to the Germans [Moravians]. I had long before observed the great seriousness of their behavior. Of their humility they had given a continual proof by performing those servile offices for the other passengers which none of the English would undertake; . . . If they were pushed, struck, or thrown down, they rose again and went away; but no complaint was found in their mouth. (Wesley's Journal, 1: 142. quoted in Howard Snyder, *The Radical Wesley* [Downers Grove, Ill.: InterVarsity Press, 1980], p. 26.)

But now, 250 years later, who has ever heard of these faithful men and women?

From Timothy's mother and grandmother in the first century (2 Tim 1:3; 3:14-15) to Eric Liddell in the twentieth century, history abounds with such little-known men and women of faith who by their exemplary, Christlike character shaped the history of the church while remaining behind the scenes.

This study guide is designed to awaken us to the character of a true disciple and move us to hunger and thirst after righteousness. The effectiveness of our deeds in the world is determined by the holiness of our lives. But today our standard is often far too mediocre, a standard which has been lowered to enable us to live comfortably. Jesus, however, calls us to live in a Christian counterculture which speaks a prophetic message to the world by its very existence.

These twelve inductive Bible studies are designed to help us grow in godly character. Several studies deal with basic yet profound truths undergirding the Christian life (such as justification and lordship). Others focus on those qualities which characterize the life of a disciple (holiness, faith, servanthood). Still others explore specific and often-neglected topics related to Christian character (such as temptation, self-image and spiritual gifts).

Through contact with the living Christ, the character of men and women throughout history has been transformed. John, a son of thunder, became the apostle of love. Paul, a hardened persecutor of God's people, gradually took on the gentleness of "a mother caring for her little children" (1 Thessalonians 2:7). May these studies bring you into vital contact with our heavenly Father who promises to conform us to the image of his Son.

Suggestions for Individual Study

1. As you begin each study, pray that God will speak to you through his Word.

2. Read the introduction to the study and respond to the personal reflection question or exercise. This is designed to help you focus on God and on the theme of the study.

3. Each study deals with a particular passage—so that you can delve into the author's meaning in that context. Read and reread the passage to be studied. If you are studying a book, it will be helpful to read through the entire book prior to the first study. The questions are written using the language of the New International Version, so you may wish to use that version of the Bible. The New Revised Standard Version is also recommended.

4. This is an inductive Bible study, designed to help you discover for yourself what Scripture is saying. The study includes three types of questions. *Observation* questions ask about the basic facts: who, what when, where and how. *Interpretation* questions delve into the meaning of the passage. *Application* questions help you discover the implications of the text for growing in Christ. These three keys unlock the treasures of Scripture.

Write your answers to the questions in the spaces provided or in a personal journal. Writing can bring clarity and deeper understanding of yourself and of God's Word.

5. It might be good to have a Bible dictionary handy. Use it to look up any unfamiliar words, names or places.

6. Use the prayer suggestion to guide you in thanking God for what you have learned and to pray about the applications that have come to mind.

7. You may want to go on to the suggestion under "Now or Later," or you may want to use that idea for your next study.

Suggestions for Members of a Group Study

1. Come to the study prepared. Follow the suggestions for individual study mentioned above. You will find that careful preparation will greatly enrich your time spent in group discussion.

2. Be willing to participate in the discussion. The leader of your group will not be lecturing. Instead, he or she will be encouraging the members of the group to discuss what they have learned. The leader will be asking the questions that are found in this guide.

3. Stick to the topic being discussed. Your answers should be based on the verses which are the focus of the discussion and not on outside authorities such as commentaries or speakers. These studies focus on a particular passage of Scripture. Only rarely should you refer to other portions of the Bible. This allows for everyone to participate in in-depth study on equal ground.

4. Be sensitive to the other members of the group. Listen attentively when they describe what they have learned. You may be surprised by their insights! Each question assumes a variety of answers. Many questions do not have "right" answers, particularly questions that aim at meaning or application. Instead the questions push us to explore the passage more thoroughly.

When possible, link what you say to the comments of others. Also, be affirming whenever you can. This will encourage some of the more hesitant members of the group to participate.

5. Be careful not to dominate the discussion. We are sometimes so eager to express our thoughts that we leave too little opportunity for others to respond. By all means participate! But allow others to also.

6. Expect God to teach you through the passage being discussed and through the other members of the group. Pray that you will have an enjoyable and profitable time together, but also that as a result of the study you will find ways that you can take action individually and/or as a group.

7. Remember that anything said in the group is considered confidential and should not be discussed outside the group unless specific permission is given to do so.

8. If you are the group leader, you will find additional suggestions at the back of the guide.

1

Freed to Serve God

Romans 3:9-26

We all have a need for acceptance. In fact our self-concept is often determined by the approval or rejection of those around us, whether family, peers, business associates, fellow students or even Christian friends. We tend to do and say what we hope will win people's favor.

GROUP DISCUSSION. What kinds of things have you done to try to earn someone's favor? Perhaps you can recall a humorous incident from your dating life or a way you tried to gain favor with a schoolteacher.

PERSONAL REFLECTION. This tendency to try to earn favor often carries over into our relationship with God. What are some ways you have tried to earn God's approval?

If we feel we must somehow earn God's acceptance of us, we end up acting out of a sense of guilt. In the book of Romans, Paul expounds the doctrine of justification, the biblical foundation upon which a right relationship is built—with ourselves, with others and with God. It frees us to be all that God intends for us. *Read Romans 3:9-26.*

1. In verses 10-18 Paul cites several Old Testament passages to illustrate the fact that everyone is "under sin" (v. 9). What portrait of humanity emerges from these verses?

---

2. How does this compare with the way you view people?

---

3. How does Paul use the various parts of the body to illustrate graphically the extent and effects of sin (vv. 13-18)?

---

4. The terminology Paul uses in this passage comes from the Roman legal system. In this courtroom scene God is the judge who is evaluating men and women on the basis of their obedience to his law. What do verses 19-20 tell us about the nature and outcome of this trial?

---

5. What do verses 9-20 reveal about our moral and spiritual condition?

---

6. Verses 21-26 introduce several key words which help us to understand the nature of salvation. A *justified* person (v. 24) has no legal charges against him or her and is therefore *righteous* in the eyes of the law. Why is our justification remarkable in light of our spiritual and moral condition?

7. How will a proper understanding of what God has done for you in Christ affect the way you view yourself?

---

8. The word *redemption* (v. 24) is borrowed from the slave market. It means to buy someone out of slavery. What are some of the ways we were enslaved as non-Christians?

---

9. What are some of the forms of enslavement or bondage that we struggle with as Christians?

How can Jesus free us in areas we continue to struggle with?

---

10. The expression *sacrifice of atonement* (v. 25) is taken from the Old Testament sacrificial system. The death of a sacrificial animal turned away God's wrath from the sinner. How does this imagery help us to understand and appreciate what Jesus did for us on the cross?

---

11. How can the fact that God has accepted and forgiven us through Christ affect our relationships with one another and with God?

Take time now to praise God for his loving and costly acceptance of us through Christ.

Now or Later

Read Romans 8:14-16. Here we see that Christ not only justifies us, that is declares us "not guilty," but he also adopts us into his family. Adoption (another legal term) is fundamentally not a change in nature but a change in status. Reflect on the implications of your new status—not an orphan or a slave but a son or daughter.

2

Acknowledging Jesus as Lord

Colossians 1:15-23

To some, Jesus of Nazareth is a revolutionary, leading the masses in their struggle for freedom from oppression. Others see him as a staunch conservative, fully supporting and representing the status quo. Still others view Jesus as a pious, meek and mild do-gooder who loves everyone and avoids confrontation at all costs.

GROUP DISCUSSION. How did you view Jesus before you became a Christian?

PERSONAL REFLECTION. How has your picture of Jesus changed? Praise God for the privilege of knowing Jesus.

What is Jesus really like? Confusion about the identity and character of Jesus was also a problem in the first century. From both inside and outside the church, distortions of the truth about Jesus and the Christian life had arisen. Against this background Paul writes to the Christians at Colossae, reminding them of who it is they follow as Lord. *Read Colossians 1:15-23.*

---

1. What characteristics of Jesus Christ impress you in this passage?

2. According to verse 15, "Christ is the visible expression of the invisible God" (Phillips). What are some of the difficulties we have in trying to know and relate to an invisible God?

How has Christ's incarnation (God becoming a human being) overcome these difficulties?

---

3. Christ is also "the firstborn," which means the one who is first (or Lord) over all creation (v. 15). In what ways are his lordship and supremacy indicated in verses 16-20?

---

4. How does this portrait of Christ enlarge your view of him?

---

5. According to verse 16, what is the purpose of all created things: nature, people, "rulers" and "authorities"?

How should this affect our attitude toward life including our possessions, relationships and goals?

---

6. Christ is also "the head of the body, the church" (v.18). How can Christ's authority make a visible difference in your church or fellowship group?

---

7. How does verse 20 help us to understand God's overall plan and goal for the universe?

---

8. According to verses 21-22, what has God done to enable us to participate in his plan?

What kind of response does he expect from us (v. 23)?

---

9. Verse 18 summarizes the overall thrust of this passage: "So that in everything he might have the supremacy." In what areas does Jesus not yet have first place in your life?

What steps can you take to submit these areas to his lordship?

---

10. How can this passage encourage you to "continue in your faith, established and firm, not moved from the hope held out in the gospel" (v. 23)?

Spend time worshiping Jesus for who he is and/or asking God for a clearer vision of him.

Now or Later

Read Revelation 4 and 5 during the week asking God to give you a fuller picture of who Jesus is.

3

The Cost of Commitment

Luke 14:25-35

Over one billion people today—almost one-fourth of the world's population—call themselves Christians. In the first century, too, multitudes flocked to Jesus. They came for various reasons and with various expectations: to satisfy curiosity, to be healed, to sit at the feet of this eloquent and controversial rabbi or simply to go along with the crowd.

GROUP DISCUSSION. What about Jesus initially attracted you to him?

PERSONAL REFLECTION. Picture yourself sitting at Jesus' feet and learning from him. What would it be like? Journal or pray in response to our Savior who invites us to come near.

At certain times during his ministry Jesus challenged his would-be disciples with strong and sobering words about the cost of truly following him as Lord. As those who claim Jesus as our Lord, we too need to carefully weigh these words. *Read Luke 14:25-35.*

---

1. In verses 25-27 what does Jesus demand of those who would truly be his disciples?

2. The word *hate* (v. 26) is an obvious exaggeration for emphasis. In what sense are we to "hate" our family and even our own life?

---

3. A person carrying a cross in first-century Palestine was about to be executed. In this light, explain the meaning and implications of verse 27.

---

4. Imagine yourself building a tower (vv. 28-30). What types of costs would you need to consider before setting out to build?

What might keep you from finishing your task?

---

5. According to verses 31-32, what does the thoughtful king understand about battle?

---

6. What do these illustrations suggest about following Jesus (v. 33)?

---

7. Some have used verse 33 as a basis for renouncing ownership and for justifying an ascetic lifestyle or even monasticism. What is the difference between giving away everything that we have and "giving up" everything we have?

8. In New Testament times salt was used both as a preservative (to keep meat from rotting) and as a seasoning. How does this parallel our role as disciples of Jesus (vv. 34-35)?

---

9. How are those who do not wholeheartedly fulfill their commitment to follow Jesus like salt without saltiness?

---

10. Give some examples of how following Jesus could be costly for you. (Consider such areas as relationships, ambitions, finances, academics and so on.)

---

11. What one thing is God calling you to change today?

Pray that God would give you grace to genuinely follow Jesus as Lord.

Now or Later

Meditate on Matthew 13:44-46. What further motivation does Jesus give us here for serving him as Lord?

4

Resisting Temptation

Genesis 39

Perhaps nothing so persistently plagues Christians like temptation. Abraham was tempted to lie and fear. David fell prey to sexual immorality. Paul wrestled with pride. Even Jesus faced innumerable temptations.

GROUP DISCUSSION. How would you define the word *temptation*?

PERSONAL REFLECTION. Spend some time reflecting. What areas of temptation do you struggle with the most? Ask God to use this study to help you with that temptation.

In Genesis 39 we observe one man's struggle and victory over temptation. Joseph was the favored eleventh son of Jacob. His jealous brothers sold the seventeen-year-old Joseph into slavery. In Egypt he was again sold, this time to Potiphar, one of Pharaoh's officials. This passage recounts the first test for Joseph as God prepared him for the crucial role he would play in Israel's history. *Read Genesis 39.*

---

1. In a few words how would you describe each of the main characters in this text—Joseph, Potiphar and Potiphar's wife?

2. Imagine yourself in Joseph's situation. What mental, emotional and physical struggles might you experience?

---

3. How did Joseph come to be in charge of Potiphar's household (vv. 1-4)?

---

4. What were the results of Joseph being placed in this position (vv. 5-6)?

---

5. How might this position of authority, wealth and power have affected Joseph?

---

6. What do we learn about Joseph's character from verses 7-9?

---

7. What would have made this temptation from Potiphar's wife especially difficult to resist?

---

8. What can you learn about overcoming persistent temptation from Joseph's example in verses 7-12?

9. What price did Joseph pay for his obedience (vv. 13-20)?

---

10. What are the "Potiphar's wives" that persistently grab at your cloak and tempt you?

How might your refusal to succumb to them be costly?

---

11. What are some ways God has worked in your life to help you overcome temptation?

Spend time confessing your struggles and sins.

Now or Later

Read Ephesians 6:10-20. What additional weapons has God given us to resist temptation? What else do you learn about spiritual warfare from this passage? Ask God to protect you.

5

Trusting God

Genesis 22:1-19

Sometimes it seems that to trust or obey God would lead to disaster. In certain instances speaking the truth, maintaining financial integrity, remaining sexually pure or faithful run counter to our basic instincts or human reasoning.

GROUP DISCUSSION. Make a list of people that you consider trustworthy. For each person you list think of an example of how you have actually put your trust in him or her. Tell the group about one of these examples.

PERSONAL REFLECTION. When is it hard for you to trust God?

Suppose God asked you to do something that seemed utterly foolish or even contrary to all that you understand God to be. How would you respond? For example, what if God asked you to kill your child? Unthinkable? Yet in Genesis 22 God places Abraham in just such a position. In this vivid and dramatic narrative, among the most beautiful in the Old Testament, we observe Abraham coming face to face with the supreme test of his faith in God. *Read Genesis 22:1-19.*

1. Describe Abraham's predicament and his response.

---

2. How would you feel if God asked you to give up the most important person in your life?

---

3. What words and phrases in verses 1-2 emphasize the extremely painful nature of God's command to Abraham?

---

4. Why would this command seem so incomprehensible to Abraham (see 17:15-22)?

---

5. List the specific ways in which Abraham demonstrates faith in verses 1-10.

---

6. In verses 11-18 the angel of the Lord calls out to Abraham twice. How would the angel's words and actions have deepened Abraham's faith?

---

7. From Abraham's example in this passage, how would you define faith?

8. How did Abraham's faith have far-reaching consequences on other people (vv. 15-18)?

9. In what ways does your faith, or lack of it, affect people around you?

10. What did Abraham learn about God from this experience?

11. What tests of faith are confronting you today?

12. How can Abraham's example encourage you to trust God more fully?

Pray that God would give you courage to trust him even when you can't fully understand what he is doing in your life.

Now or Later

Read James 1:2-5. Reflect on God's purposes in testing us.

6

Living Holy Lives

Ephesians 4:17—5:7

For many people the word *holiness* conjures up images of a self-righteous person who is totally removed from the problems of the world, talks only about "spiritual things" and is serious and even sullen in appearance. Yet the New Testament word *holy* is used to describe God's people in general and not a select few.

GROUP DISCUSSION. People often view pastors, priests, missionaries and full-time Christian workers as more holy than other Christians. Why do you think this is so?

PERSONAL REFLECTION. How do you feel about studying holiness?

Holiness is the goal of the Christian's life and is fundamental to witness and service in the world. Robert Murray McCheyne has written that a holy person is "an awesome weapon in the hand of God." In this light, we need to recapture the biblical call to holy living. Read Ephesians 4:17—5:7.

1. In verses 17-19 Paul describes how the Gentiles live. How does he characterize their minds, hearts and practices?

2. How does this description compare with the world you experience every day? Explain.

---

3. In contrast to the non-Christians described in verses 17-19, how were the Ephesians taught to live as Christians (vv. 20-24)?

---

4. Putting off our old self and putting on the new is a way of describing what happens when we become Christians. How does this description shed light on the nature of conversion?

---

5. If you are to become like God in true righteousness and holiness (v. 24), why is it essential for you to "be made new in the attitude of your mind" (v. 23)?

---

6. In practical terms, what can we do to renew our minds?

---

7. Because of our new identity in Christ, what things must be put away, and what things ought to take their place (vv. 25-32)?

8. With each command in verses 25-32, explain the reason Paul calls us to live differently.

9. How can we imitate God and Christ in our relationships with others (5:1-2)?

10. Why is it "improper" and "out of place" for God's holy people to do the things mentioned in verses 3-4?

Which of these do you have the greatest difficulty avoiding? Explain.

11. Looking back over this passage, what different areas of our life are to be affected by holiness?

12. What type of behavior do you most need to put off and put on, and what steps can you take to change this area of your life?

Pray that the Holy Spirit would give you an increasing desire to be like Christ.

Now or Later

Read Isaiah 6 noting how Isaiah responds to the holiness of God.

7

Showing Compassion

Luke 10:25-37

"All men will know that you are my disciples if you love one another." Tertullian, an early church theologian, boasted in one of his works that this statement of Jesus had become a fact. Even their enemies, writes Tertullian, marveled: "look how they love one another."

GROUP DISCUSSION. Think of a Christian you consider compassionate. What stands out to you about that person?

PERSONAL REFLECTION. Who has shown you compassion? Praise God for that person's grace in your life.

Unfortunately the church has not always been marked by compassion and self-sacrifice. Far too often we speak of love but fail to back our words with deeds of kindness and mercy. We need to drink deeply from the simple but profound message of the story of the good Samaritan. Its familiarity has so weakened its impact that it is seen as an exception rather than the norm for the citizens of the kingdom of God. As you read this passage, imagine that you are hearing it from Jesus himself for the first time. *Read Luke 10:25-37.*

---

1. In your own words recount the context and the content of this parable.

2. What do you learn in verses 25-29 about the expert in the law?

---

3. The expert in the law quotes from Deuteronomy 6:5 and Leviticus 19:18. How do these two commands summarize the essence of what God desires in our lives?

---

4. In reply to the question "Who is my neighbor?" Jesus tells a story (vv. 30-35). Describe a modern-day equivalent of this incident.

---

5. Suggest possible reasons why the priests and Levites may have passed by on the other side.

---

6. What are some ways we tend to pass by those in need?

---

7. Describe the Samaritan's involvement with the man from the moment he sees him (vv. 33-35).

---

8. Considering the racial and religious tensions that existed between Jews and Samaritans, why is the response of the Samaritan particularly surprising?

9. How have you personally been involved with people who are hurting financially, emotionally, physically or socially?

---

10. How does the extent of the Samaritan's involvement compare with most attempts we make to help needy people?

---

11. How has the story of the good Samaritan challenged the lawyer's understanding of "love your neighbor as yourself" (vv. 36-37)?

---

12. What things keep you from not only seeing but also acting in response to the needs of those around you?

How can you begin to be more of a neighbor to these people?

Pray that God would show you one person whom you can love as a neighbor this week.

Now or Later

Read Matthew 25:31-46. What light does this passage shed on the importance of living compassionately?

8

Serving Others

Philippians 2

Power. Glory. Success. Throughout human history these have captured the hearts of men and women. In the midst of a society which measures worth by position and wealth, it is no wonder that Christians have struggled to stand for the values of the kingdom of God: humility, self-denial, gentleness, love. In the eyes of the world these are often signs of weakness rather than strength.

GROUP DISCUSSION. What images come to your mind when you hear the word *servant*? Is it positive or negative? Explain.

PERSONAL DISCUSSION. In what ways do you struggle with seeing yourself as a servant?

In stark contrast to the values of our day, Jesus came not to be served but to serve. He calls us to follow in his steps. *Read Philippians* 2.

---

1. What themes connect Jesus, Timothy and Epaphroditus in this passage?

2. How is verse 1 an incentive to obey Paul's commands in verse 2?

---

3. How do Paul's commands in verses 3-4 go against our natural tendencies?

How do they go against the spirit of our society?

---

4. How is Christ the supreme example of the humility and servanthood described in verses 3-4?

---

5. What did it cost him to be a servant (vv. 6-8)?

---

6. In verses 12-18 Paul exhorts the Philippians to live godly lives. In what way is he a model of servanthood for them?

---

7. How does Paul contrast Timothy with others (vv. 20-21)?

---

8. If Timothy were alive today, how might his "genuine interest" in the church's welfare be manifested in practical ways?

---

9. How has Epaphroditus been a servant to Paul and the Philippians (vv. 25-30)?

---

10. Jesus said, "The Son of Man did not come to be served, but to serve" (Mark 10:45). Paul, Timothy and Epaphroditus demonstrated the same kind of lifestyle. What are some ways you might follow their example more fully today or this week?

How can you serve others joyfully without getting "burned out"?

Pray that God would give you grace to serve in practical ways in the coming week.

Now or Later

Read John 13:1-17. What additional insights does this passage provide?

9

Developing a Godly Self-Image

Exodus 3:1-15; 4:1-17

Few people today are immune to the effects of our fragmented, impersonal and fiercely competitive society. Many of us, both inside and outside the church, have been bruised by broken families and relationships. These wounds have not only damaged our self-images but have also hindered us from responding fully to God's love and purposes for our lives.

GROUP DISCUSSION. Why do you think so many people struggle with a poor self-image?

PERSONAL REFLECTION. Bring your own self-image struggles and questions to God in prayer.

Moses, like many today, felt insignificant and inadequate. He had been raised in the courts of the king of Egypt in great wealth and with the best of education and training. But witnessing an act of unrighteousness against a fellow Jew, Moses took matters into his own hands and killed a man. As a result he was forced to flee to Midian, where he spent the next forty years herding sheep. At the beginning of Exodus 3 he is eighty years old and has accomplished very little in his life. *Read Exodus 3:1-15 and 4:1-17.*

---

1. Describe the setting in 3:1-3.

2. In 3:4 God calls Moses by name. What does this tell Moses about God?

---

3. Why does God send Moses to Pharaoh (3:7-10)?

---

4. In 3:11-15 Moses raises two objections against his going to Pharaoh. What do these objections reveal about Moses' view of himself and God?

---

5. In what situations do you feel inadequate to do what God commands or desires?

How can God's reply to Moses encourage you (3:12, 14-15)?

---

6. Moses gives his third objection in 4:1. How does God reassure him in 4:2-9?

---

7. What are some of the resources God has given you to accomplish his will in a difficult or fearful area?

---

8. In 4:10 Moses claims that he lacks the gifts to serve God effectively.

How does his view of himself differ from God's perspective (4:11-12)?

---

9. When is it legitimate to admit that we are unqualified for an area of service, and when is it merely a faithless excuse?

---

10. In what way can a poor self-image become sin (4:13-17)?

---

11. In what areas do you allow your self-image to be determined by your emotions or by other people rather than by God and his Word? Explain.

---

12. According to this passage, how should our self-image be affected by our image of God?

Pray for one another's emotional healing and for grace to move forward as Moses did.

Now or Later

If you don't already, begin to keep a journal on a regular basis. Try to express in writing this week some of your feelings or struggles as you reflect on this passage.

10

Using Your Spiritual Gifts

1 Corinthians 12:4-26

Tongues, prophecy, teaching, evangelism, mercy. In recent years a wide spectrum of views has developed among Christians about spiritual gifts. In *Fire in the Fireplace* Charles Hummel describes a common misconception: "Christians are often urged to inquire: 'What is *my* gift? How can I discover and use it?' Our culture pressures us to ask: 'Who am I? How can I be fulfilled and realize my potential?' " But is this the emphasis of the New Testament's teaching on spiritual gifts?

GROUP DISCUSSION. How does your view of yourself affect the way you interact with other Christians?

PERSONAL REFLECTION. Pray that God will help you to understand your spiritual gifts.

Questions and confusion about spiritual gifts prevailed in the church at Corinth. In 1 Corinthians 12—14 Paul discusses the nature, purpose and use of spiritual gifts as a corrective to the abuses which had arisen. *Read 1 Corinthians 12:4-26.*

---

1. In what ways can our entire body be hindered if one of its parts isn't functioning properly?

2. In verses 4-11 what do we learn about the similarities and differences among spiritual gifts?

3. What is the purpose of the gifts?

4. How does Paul respond to the misconceptions in verses 15-16?

5. How do the people described in verse 21 view themselves and those with less "spectacular" gifts?

6. In contrast to verse 21, how should we view and treat those who seem to be weaker or less honorable (vv. 22-23)?

Where do you see examples of this in your church or fellowship group?

7. Why would the "presentable parts" of the body need no special treatment (v. 24)?

8. If the more "spectacular" members of the body don't need special treatment, why are they usually the first to receive it?

9. How does this passage correct some of our misconceptions about the difference between so-called "full-time Christian workers" and everyone else?

10. Comment on your understanding of your own place in the body of Christ. For instance, do you feel inferior? Superior? Unsure of how you fit? Are you a lone ranger?

11. According to 12:7, each Christian is given gifts "for the common good" of the body. In this light, what can you be doing to build up your local church or fellowship group?

Pray that God will fill each of you with the love of Jesus as you use your spiritual gifts.

Now or Later

For further study of spiritual gifts, examine the four primary passages in Scripture where gifts are discussed: Romans 12, 1 Corinthians 12, Ephesians 4 and 1 Peter 4. Each of these contributes to our overall understanding of spiritual gifts.

11

Greatness Through Humility

Mark 10:32-45

Pride comes in all shapes and sizes. Some of us put ourselves on a pedestal from which we judge the faults of everyone else. Others are so self-effacing that they cannot take their eyes off themselves and their own inadequacies. Still others swing like a pendulum from one extreme to the other.

GROUP DISCUSSION. What is the difference between humility and a poor self-image?

PERSONAL REFLECTION. Reflect on Jesus' humility. Spend time in prayer asking God to use this study to build a little more of Jesus' character in you.

Paul exhorts us neither to exalt nor to belittle ourselves, but rather to think of ourselves with sober judgment (Romans 12:3). In Mark 10 we see that the disciples too were constantly learning to live humbly like the Lord Jesus. *Read Mark 10:32-45.*

---

1. Describe the basic tension here between James and John on the one hand and Jesus on the other.

2. What does Jesus tell his disciples about what awaits him in Jerusalem (vv. 32-34)?

---

3. In light of this news, how is the request of James and John inappropriate (v. 35)?

---

4. In ways are you like James and John in this passage?

---

5. The words *baptism* and *cup* in verses 38-39 are sometimes used symbolically in Scripture to denote suffering. In this context, explain Jesus' reply to James and John.

---

6. Compare the sin of the other ten disciples with that of James and John (v. 41).

---

7. Have you ever felt envious or even indignant when others were honored and you were not? Explain.

---

8. How does Jesus contrast greatness in the world with greatness in God's kingdom (vv. 42-45)?

9. What is radical about his definition of greatness?

---

10. In what ways do Christians today still embrace the world's concept of greatness?

---

11. Give a positive example of humility in action that you've seen in your church, family or work.

---

12. Jesus' concept of greatness and humility could transform every area of our lives. Name one way you could begin to follow his example.

Pray that God the Holy Spirit would help you not just to do humble acts to be humble like Jesus.

Now or Later

Read 2 Corinthians 12:1-10. What does God do to keep Paul humble? What are some ways he might be doing this in your life?

12

Called to Persevere

2 Timothy 1:8—2:7

Sometimes following Jesus is more than we bargained for. We wonder may why God allows bad things to happen to us while others seem to have an easy life. Sometimes we feel like simply quitting.

GROUP DISCUSSION. Have you ever felt like giving up Christianity and taking up an easier way of life? Explain.

PERSONAL REFLECTION. What aspects of Christianity feel like weighty demands or burdens to you?

As a young and timid leader, Timothy faced the dual dilemma of personal inadequacy and a problem-stricken church. If that weren't enough, Paul, his father in the faith, was in prison facing the prospect of death. His arrest evidently resulted in widespread defections from the faith. This is the last letter Paul wrote before he was executed. From his cell he challenges Timothy to endure. *Read 2 Timothy 1:8—2:7.*

---

1. What basic facts do we learn from this passage about Paul, Timothy and the relationship between the two?

2. Why might Timothy be ashamed to testify about the Lord or be ashamed of Paul (v. 8)?

---

3. After calling Timothy to suffer with him for the gospel, what specific truths does Paul focus on (1:9-10) and why?

---

4. How does the message of the gospel encourage you to stand firm when you are tempted to be ashamed of Christ or of another Christian?

---

5. What do verses 13-14 suggest about the difficulties Timothy will encounter?

---

6. Imagine yourself in Paul's position—alone, imprisoned, deserted by "everyone in the province of Asia" (1:15). How do you think you would react?

---

7. What is distinctive about Onesiphorus (1:16-18)?

---

8. Against the background of Paul's impending death and the disloyalty of the Asian church, what is the significance of Paul's command in 2:2?

9. Reflect on the three metaphors describing the Christian life (2:3-6). How does each provide insight into the life of a disciple?

---

10. In each illustration, what are the consequences for the person who fails to endure?

---

11. In what specific ways might it cost you to endure for the sake of the gospel, both now and throughout your life?

---

12. Timothy was undoubtedly overwhelmed by his own inadequacy and the massive defections from the church. How would 2:1 encourage him in the face of the great task at hand?

How is it an encouragement to you?

Pray for the strength and grace to persevere in any difficult circumstances you or others in your group are facing.

Now or Later

Read Hebrew 12:1-3. How is the example of faithful Christian men and women of the past an encouragement to you to persevere?

Leader's Notes

MY GRACE IS SUFFICIENT FOR YOU. (2 COR 12:9)

Leading a Bible discussion can be an enjoyable and rewarding experience. But it can also be *scary*—especially if you've never done it before. If this is your feeling, you're in good company. When God asked Moses to lead the Israelites out of Egypt, he replied, "O Lord, please send someone else to do it!" (Ex 4:13). It was the same with Solomon, Jeremiah and Timothy, but God helped these people in spite of their weaknesses, and he will help you as well.

You don't need to be an expert on the Bible or a trained teacher to lead a Bible discussion. The idea behind these inductive studies is that the leader guides group members to discover for themselves what the Bible has to say. This method of learning will allow group members to remember much more of what is said than a lecture would.

These studies are designed to be led easily. As a matter of fact, the flow of questions through the passage from observation to interpretation to application is so natural that you may feel that the studies lead themselves. This study guide is also flexible. You can use it with a variety of groups—student, professional, neighborhood or church groups. Each study takes forty-five to sixty minutes in a group setting.

There are some important facts to know about group dynamics and encouraging discussion. The suggestions listed below should enable you to effectively and enjoyably fulfill your role as leader.

Preparing for the Study

1. Ask God to help you understand and apply the passage in your own life. Unless this happens, you will not be prepared to lead others. Pray too for the various members of the group. Ask God to open your hearts to the message of his Word and motivate you to action.

2. Read the introduction to the entire guide to get an overview of the entire book and the issues which will be explored.

3. As you begin each study, read and reread the assigned Bible passage to familiarize yourself with it.

4. This study guide is based on the New International Version of the Bible. It will help you and the group if you use this translation as the basis for your study and discussion.

5. Carefully work through each question in the study. Spend time in meditation and reflection as you consider how to respond.

6. Write your thoughts and responses in the space provided in the study guide. This will help you to express your understanding of the passage clearly.

7. It might help to have a Bible dictionary handy. Use it to look up any unfamiliar words, names or places. (For additional help on how to study a passage, see chapter five of *How to Lead a LifeGuide Bible Study*, InterVarsity Press.)

8. Consider how you can apply the Scripture to your life. Remember that the group will follow your lead in responding to the studies. They will not go any deeper than you do.

9. Once you have finished your own study of the passage, familiarize yourself with the leader's notes for the study you are leading. These are designed to help you in several ways. First, they tell you the purpose the study guide author had in mind when writing the study. Take time to think through how the study questions work together to accomplish that purpose. Second, the notes provide you with additional background information or suggestions on group dynamics for various questions. This information can be useful when people have difficulty understanding or answering a question. Third, the leader's notes can alert you to potential problems you may encounter during the study.

10. If you wish to remind yourself of anything mentioned in the leader's notes, make a note to yourself below that question in the study.

Leading the Study

1. Begin the study on time. Open with prayer, asking God to help the group to understand and apply the passage.

2. Be sure that everyone in your group has a study guide. Encourage the

group to prepare beforehand for each discussion by reading the introduction to the guide and by working through the questions in the study.

3. At the beginning of your first time together, explain that these studies are meant to be discussions, not lectures. Encourage the members of the group to participate. However, do not put pressure on those who may be hesitant to speak during the first few sessions. You may want to suggest the following guidelines to your group.

☐ Stick to the topic being discussed.

☐ Your responses should be based on the verses which are the focus of the discussion and not on outside authorities such as commentaries or speakers.

☐ These studies focus on a particular passage of Scripture. Only rarely should you refer to other portions of the Bible. This allows for everyone to participate in in-depth study on equal ground.

☐ Anything said in the group is considered confidential and will not be discussed outside the group unless specific permission is given to do so.

☐ We will listen attentively to each other and provide time for each person present to talk.

☐ We will pray for each other.

4. Have a group member read the introduction at the beginning of the discussion.

5. Every session begins with a group discussion question. The question or activity is meant to be used before the passage is read. The question introduces the theme of the study and encourages group members to begin to open up. Encourage as many members as possible to participate and be ready to get the discussion going with your own response.

This section is designed to reveal where our thoughts or feelings need to be transformed by Scripture. That is why it is especially important not to read the passage before the discussion question is asked. The passage will tend to color the honest reactions people would otherwise give because they are, of course, supposed to think the way the Bible does.

You may want to supplement the group discussion question with an icebreaker to help people to get comfortable. See the community section of *Small Group Idea Book* for more ideas.

You also might want to use the personal reflection question with your group. Either allow a time of silence for people to respond individually or discuss it together.

6. Have a group member (or members if the passage is long) read aloud the passage to be studied. Then give people several minutes to read the passage again silently so that they can take it all in.

7. Question 1 will generally be an overview question designed to briefly survey the passage. Encourage the group to briefly survey the passage, but try to avoid getting sidetracked by questions or issues that will be addressed later in the study.

8. As you ask the questions, keep in mind that they are designed to be used just as they are written. You may simply read them aloud. Or you may prefer to express them in your own words.

There may be times when it is appropriate to deviate from the study guide. For example, a question may have already been answered. If so, move on to the next question. Or someone may raise an important question not covered in the guide. Take time to discuss it, but try to keep the group from going off on tangents.

9. Avoid answering your own questions. If necessary, repeat or rephrase them until they are clearly understood. Or point out something you read in the leader's notes to clarify the context or meaning. An eager group quickly becomes passive and silent if they think the leader will do most of the talking.

10. Don't be afraid of silence. People may need time to think about the question before formulating their answers.

11. Don't be content with just one answer. Ask, "What do the rest of you think?" or "Anything else?" until several people have given answers to the question.

12. Acknowledge all contributions. Try to be affirming whenever possible. Never reject an answer. If it is clearly off-base, ask, "Which verse led you to that conclusion?" or again, "What do the rest of you think?"

13. Don't expect every answer to be addressed to you, even though this will probably happen at first. As group members become more at ease, they will begin to truly interact with each other. This is one sign of healthy discussion.

14. Don't be afraid of controversy. It can be very stimulating. If you don't resolve an issue completely, don't be frustrated. Move on and keep it in mind for later. A subsequent study may solve the problem.

15. Periodically summarize what the group has said about the passage. This helps to draw together the various ideas mentioned and gives continuity to the study. But don't preach.

16. At the end of the Bible discussion you may want to allow group members a time of quiet to work on an idea under "Now or Later." Then discuss what you experienced. Or you may want to encourage group members to work on these ideas between meetings. Give an opportunity during the session to allow people to talk about what they are learning.

17. Conclude your time together with conversational prayer, adapting the prayer suggestion at the end of the study to your group. Ask for God's help in following through on the commitments you've made.

18. End on time.

Many more suggestions and helps are found in *How to Lead a LifeGuide Bible Study,* which is part of the LifeGuide Bible Study series.

Components of Small Groups

A healthy small group should do more than study the Bible. There are four components to consider as you structure your time together.

Nurture. Small groups help us to grow in our knowledge and love of God. Bible study is the key to making this happen and is the foundation of your small group.

Community. Small groups are a great place to develop deep friendships with other Christians. Allow time for informal interaction before and after each study. Plan activities and games that will help you to get to know each other. Spend time having fun together—going on a picnic or cooking dinner together.

Worship and prayer. Your study will be enhanced by spending time praising God together in prayer or song. Pray for each other's needs—and keep track of how God is answering prayer in your group. Ask God to help you to apply what you are learning in your study.

Outreach. Reaching out to others can be a practical way of applying what you are learning, and it will keep your group from becoming self-focused. Host a series of evangelistic discussions for your friends or neighbors. Clean up the yard of an elderly friend. Serve at a soup kitchen together, or spend a day working on a Habitat house.

Many more suggestions and helps in each of these areas are found in

Small Group Idea Book. Information on building a small group can be found in *Small Group Leaders' Handbook* and *The Big Book on Small Groups* (both from InterVarsity Press). Reading through one of these books would be worth your time.

Study 1. Freed to Serve God. Romans 3:9-26.
Purpose: To understand why God accepts us and how this acceptance should affect our attitude toward ourselves, others and God.
Personal reflection. If you are leading a group, you can either skip these questions or allow people time to silently reflect on them to help them open up to God as the study begins. The purpose of this specific question is to help us recognize subtle ways in which we live by works rather than by grace. For example, after we sin we sometimes try to make payment for that sin ourselves, perhaps by spending an extra half-hour in prayer, doing an "extra" good deed and so on.
Question 1. It might be helpful to understand the context of this study. In Romans 1:18—3:20 Paul describes everyone's condition apart from Jesus Christ. These chapters demonstrate that "no one will be declared righteous in his [God's] sight by observing the law" (3:20). Then in 3:21—5:21 Paul describes the "righteousness from God [which] comes through faith in Jesus Christ" (3:22).

Paul's portrait is drawn from the characteristics of humanity in general. Not everyone has reached the depths of depravity described here, but everyone is capable of reaching such depths because our nature is fallen.
Question 3. The group may have already answered this question while discussing question 1. If so, move on to the next question. However, their answer to question 1 may have been fairly general. Question 3 allows them to be more specific as they look at Paul's portrait of fallen humanity.
Question 6. Questions 6-10 will look at each of these key words, one at a time. Verses 21-26 are central to the study. You need to understand and be gripped by the deep significance of the cross if you expect it to make an impact on others. A Bible dictionary can help you define key words.
Question 7. Help the group to see the connection between God's high view of us in Christ and how we ought to view ourselves.
Question 9. Christians may struggle with the same temptations as non-Christians, but consider also the more subtle inward temptations: the drive

for success, approval, power or wealth.

Question 10. Some people object to the idea of God's wrath being turned away by the death of a sacrificial victim. In their opinion this makes God too similar to pagan deities who could be bribed. Yet in paganism the worshiper tries desperately to appease the gods' wrath. In Christianity God himself graciously provided and even became the sacrificial victim.

Question 11. Ask the group to first consider our relationships with one another, then our relationship with God.

Study 2. Acknowledging Jesus as Lord. Colossians 1:15-23.

Purpose: To understand the significance of the person and work of Christ.

Question 1. If several people in your group became Christians as children, you might want to change the question to "How do you think your non-Christian friends view Jesus Christ?"

Question 2. Concerning Christ's incarnation, F. F. Bruce writes: "It may be observed in passing that there is a close association between the doctrine of man's creation in the divine image and the doctrine of our Lord's incarnation; it is because man in the creative order bears the image of his Creator that it was possible for the Son of God to become incarnate as man and in His humanity to display the glory of the invisible God" (*Ephesians and Colossians*, The New International Commentary on the New Testament [Grand Rapids, Mich.: Eerdmans, 1973], p. 194).

Question 3. The term *firstborn* is commonly used to mean "supreme" or "sovereign." It is a synonym for "most exalted of the kings of the earth" (see Ps 89:27).

Question 5. Many people know that all things were created by Jesus Christ and for him, but few have meditated on the personal implications of this fact. If the group needs help with the second part of the question, you might point them to Christ's ownership of all creation—including us—and what this suggests about our rights.

Question 8. Someone may raise a question as to whether verse 23 is teaching that we can lose our salvation. While Paul is confident that the Colossians will remain firm in the faith, he inserts a conditional clause to emphasize their need to persevere. The thrust of the Bible teaches that all true Christians will endure to the end. However, this passage and others indicate that believers are not immune to the dangers of apostasy.

Question 9. Be sure to leave time for this question. It helps the group to apply the main theme of the passage.

Study 3. The Cost of Commitment. Luke 14:25-35.

Purpose: To evaluate one's life in light of the lordship of Christ and to give Christ control of one uncommitted area.

General Note. The InterVarsity Press booklet *My Heart—Christ's Home* is a helpful introduction to this study and to the topic itself. You might read it yourself before the study and recommend it to the group for further consideration.

Question 3. Matthew 10:37 helps to clarify Jesus' meaning in Luke 14:26: "Anyone who loves his father or mother more than me is not worthy of me; anyone who loves his son or daughter more than me is not worthy of me." Jesus demands to have first place in all our relationships.

Question 4. See also Luke 9:23 and Matthew 10:38. The New Testament makes it clear that suffering comes before glory, that the cross comes before the crown. In Jesus' words, we must be willing to lose our lives for his sake—that is, give up all claim to our possessions, our relationships, our ambitions and even our own lives—if we want to follow him. This must be done daily, not just once (Lk 9:23). Only then will we find life. The cost of commitment will be discussed more fully in the rest of the study, so don't feel that you must cover everything here.

Question 6. The main point of these illustrations is that we should carefully consider the cost of following Jesus before we become his disciples. Help the group to focus primarily on this idea. If they begin to go off on a tangent, ask them: "What is the main point of these illustrations? How does it relate to following Jesus?"

Question 7. There are two extremes to avoid in applying this verse. One is a wooden literalism followed by many cults. They suggest that Christ commands us to give away all our possessions and to renounce our family, friends, career and so on. Another extreme is to so spiritualize Christ's words that they are emptied of their force. Following Christ costs us everything in principle but nothing in practice! Help the group to avoid these extremes and to wrestle with the true meaning of Jesus' words.

Questions 11-12. Help the group to be specific in considering the implications of Christ's lordship. Encourage each person to identify one area which God is calling him or her to change.

As an alternative or supplement to this question you might ask, "Are there areas of your life in which you are resisting Jesus' lordship? Explain."

Study 4. Resisting Temptation. Genesis 39.

Purpose: To consider the sources of temptation and how to effectively combat them.

One problem you may face in this study is an unwillingness on the part of the group members to be really open about their struggles with temptation. Seek to create an open, accepting atmosphere. To do this you will need to be open about your own struggles with temptation. However, be careful not to put others on the spot if they are not ready to share.

Group discussion. The *American Heritage Dictionary* defines *tempt* as follows: "To entice (someone) to commit an unwise or immoral act, esp. by a promise or reward." If the group has difficulty answering this question, you might read this definition.

Question 1. Read Genesis 37 for the background to this story.

Question 3-4. We see Joseph's rise in verses 2-6. First he works indoors and not in the fields (v. 2). Then he becomes Potiphar's personal attendant (v. 4). Finally, he is put in charge of the household (v. 5). All this is because "the LORD was with Joseph" (v. 2), and it is the Lord who blesses the household (v. 5). (Gordon Wenham, *Genesis 16—50* [Dallas: Word, 1994], p. 373.)

Question 6. Gordon Wenhem notes that verses 7-10: "seem to cover a prolonged period in which Potiphar's wife tries to persuade the glamorous Joseph to lie with her. Her raw lust and his sense of propriety and loyalty are admirably captured by the dialogue. Her peremptory 'lie with me' is countered by a long speech by Joseph, showing his own sense of moral shock at the suggestion" (*Genesis 16—50,* p. 375).

Question 8. In 7-10 we see Joseph refuse her daily. He argues loyalty to her husband and to God. When she gets more aggressive (v. 12), he flees the house.

The cloak (v. 11) was not what we think of as a coat. "The main items of attire in patriarchal times were mid-calf and a tunic, a long T-shirt. . . . To pull either of these garments off against the wearer's will must have involved surprise and violence" (*Genesis 16—50,* p. 376).

Question 9. Although Joseph's imprisonment is costly and seems to be only negative at the outset, it might be noted that in Genesis 40-50 God uses this seemingly adverse situation to accomplish greater purposes through Joseph. See, for example, Genesis 50:20.

Question 10. There is often an even greater cost when we give in to temptation. David's sin with Bathsheba and subsequent murder in 2 Samuel 11 is a poignant example of the consequences of yielding to temptation. Although David was forgiven his sin, the kingdom of Israel was never the same after that. You may want to remind the group of this account for illustration.

Question 11. Encourage the group to be specific in answering this question. You may want to remind them of God's assurance to us in 1 Corinthians 10:13 as we face temptation.

Prayer. You may want to allow a time of silent prayer. You could also break into pairs and pray for each other more personally.

Study 5. Trusting God. Genesis 22:1-19.

Purpose: To understand the nature of faith and to be encouraged to trust God more fully.

Question 1. God's request here is as deeply disturbing to us as it was to the original hearers of this story. "The usual victims of burnt offerings were birds, sheep, or if the worshiper was very wealthy, a bull. But to offer one's child was quite out of the question for devout orthodox worshipers. 'Shall I give my first-born for my transgression, the fruit of my body for the sin of my soul?' asks Micah (6:7), expecting his hearers to reply with an emphatic no" (*Genesis 16—50,* p. 105).

Question 2. Encourage members of the group to enter into the story as deeply as possible.

Question 3. Take adequate time for this question. Be sure the group grasps the twofold struggle of Abraham: (1) God's command seemed to conflict with his previous promise that through Isaac the great nation of Israel would be born, and (2) his personal struggle with sacrificing his only son (vv. 2, 12, 16) for whom he had waited so many years.

Question 4. Notice in Genesis 17 how long Abraham and Sarah had waited for a child.

Question 5. In verse 3 Abraham begins his journey—the next day—he prepares the wood and takes his son. In verse 4 he stops at the place God designates. In verses 6-8 he carries the wood and the fire. In verse 9 he builds the fire. In verse 10 he prepares to kill his son.

Question 7. Hebrews 11:1 defines faith as "being sure of what we hope for and certain of what we do not see." Faith can also be described as believing and trusting that what God says is true and acting accordingly. If the group doesn't connect with the obedience aspect of faith, you might ask, "What does this passage reveal about the relationship between faith and obedience?"

Questions 9-12. Leave time for these key application questions. Attempt to think through, in advance, the various tests of faith which confront you and the members of your group during a typical week. For example, what does it mean to act in faith when a tragedy occurs, when you are tempted to sin, when you face financial difficulties or when you are ridiculed for being a Christian?

Study 6. Living Holy Lives. Ephesians 4:17—5:7.

Purpose: To understand our call to holiness and to be motivated toward godly living.

Question 1. It might be helpful for your group if you place this passage in its context. John Stott writes: "For three chapters Paul has been unfolding for his readers the eternal purpose of God being worked out in history. . . . Paul sees an alienated humanity being reconciled, a fractured humanity being united, even a new humanity being created. . . . Now the apostle moves on from the new society to the new standards which are expected of it. So he turns from exposition to exhortation, from what God has done. . . . to what we must do" (*The Message of Ephesians* [Downers Grove, Ill.: InterVarsity Press, 1979], p. 146).

Question 3. The word *holy* in Scripture usually refers to a person or thing which has been set apart for God and his service. It also denotes the purity of God's character and, secondarily, the character of his people.

Question 4. The RSV mistakenly translates *put off* and *put on* as commands. In fact, Paul is not commanding us but rather is describing what we were taught, presumably at conversion. The parallel passage in Colossians says, "Do not lie to each other, since you *have* taken off your old self with its practices and *have* put on the new self" (Col 3:9-10, our emphasis).

Because we have put off the old self and put on the new, we are commanded to live differently.

Question 5. This question relates to the issue of self-image. Our view of ourselves very much influences the way we act. Paul's argument here is that because of what God has done in Jesus Christ, we are new people with new identities. Therefore, we should be leading a radically different life than we were prior to conversion.

Question 6. This question could lead to a discussion on claiming God's promises, meditating on Scripture and so on. While these are important points for consideration, don't spend too much time on them. Remember that the focus of the study is holiness.

Question 9. Be sure to allow enough time to consider this question fully. People often fail to see that holiness should affect our relationships with others.

Question 10. Some members of your group may be troubled by Paul's warning. If we are saved by faith and not by works (2:8-9), then how could our works exclude us from God's kingdom? Paul's point is that people who live such lives give evidence that they are not God's children, regardless of what they claim.

Study 7. Showing Compassion. Luke 10:25-37.

Purpose: To understand the biblical nature of compassion and to consider how to become a better neighbor in at least one specific situation.

Question 2. An "expert in the law," or "lawyer" as it appears in some translations, was not an expert on the secular law but on the first five books of the Old Testament and on their application to secular affairs.

Question 4. The road from Jerusalem to Jericho was about seventeen miles long. It was rocky and treacherous and known for its dangers to travelers at the hands of robbers.

Question 5. You might want to mention that touching a dead person was forbidden by the ceremonial law (Lev 21:1-4). Some commentators have suggested that this may have had some bearing on their negligence. This, of course, relates to the tension between our remaining separate from the world while a part of it. However, there are many other possible explanations.

Questions 7-8. During New Testament times there was considerable hostility between Jews and Samaritans. The Jews considered the Samaritans racially and religiously impure. The Samaritans accepted only the first five books of the Old Testament (with some of their own changes). They built a rival temple on Mount Gerizim which the Jews destroyed in 128 B.C. Between A.D. 6 and 9 the Samaritans scattered bones in the Jerusalem temple during Passover (bones were considered unclean). As a result of these tensions John 4:9 states, "Jews do not associate with Samaritans." In fact, they would normally walk around Samaria rather than take the shorter route through it. All of these things help us to feel the impact of Jesus' story about the good Samaritan.

Question 9. In this question it would be easy to focus exclusively on our failures. Avoid this tendency by encouraging the group to also share positive examples of obedience from their own experience.

Question 11. Again, pace yourself well so that these critical questions of application are fully considered and the truths of the passage fully digested.

Questions 12. Encourage group members to be specific and creative here. Loving a neighbor might involve becoming vulnerable about your own life, spending time listening and entering someone else's world, writing a note of encouragement, giving practical help. The possibilities are endless.

Study 8. Serving Others. Philippians 2.

Purpose: To understand the biblical concept of servanthood so that we may better serve others.

Question 4. Verses 5-11 contain one of the most beautiful portraits of Christ found in Scripture. It is astonishing that God would be willing to become a human. It is equally surprising that he would take the form of a lowly servant rather than a wealthy monarch. But it is incomprehensible that he would be willing to be utterly humiliated by dying in the manner reserved for the worst of criminals. These few verses capture the greatness of Christ's humility and love.

Question 5. This question may or may not overlap with the previous question, depending on how fully the group answers question 4. If there is significant overlap, simply move on to the next question.

Question 6. It is important to realize that Paul is writing this letter from prison. As a result of his service to Jesus Christ and the church, he is confined under guard (possibly in Rome) and may be facing the threat of execution.

Question 8. Consider spiritual aspects of caring for others—discipling and mentoring or praying with another. Or consider the practical ways that we can care for each other by helping each other out with big jobs like moving or caring for each others' children.

Question 12. Encourage each member of the group to think of practical ways he or she can serve others during the coming week. Perhaps the group can share their experiences in applying this study at the beginning of the next study.

Study 9. Developing a Godly Self-Image. Exodus 3:1-15; 4:1-17.

Purpose: To understand how our self-image must be balanced by a proper image of God.

General note. In a sense, this is not a typical study on self-image. Normally such studies attempt to replace low self-esteem by giving us reasons for high self-esteem: we are created in God's image, we are loved and valued by God, and so on. It is important for us to grasp these things. But this passage and study take a different approach. God does not seek to correct Moses' low self-image by giving him a proper image of self but rather by giving him a proper image of God. Because God is with him, Moses' weaknesses and sense of inadequacy are not obstacles but opportunities to witness God's power, grace and sufficiency.

Question 4. Notice in 3:13 "God has not identified himself to Moses by name (see v. 6; cf. Ge. 17:1)." In 3:14 God reveals the name "which expressed his character as the dependable and faithful God who desires the full trust of his people" (*NIV Study Bible,* [Grand Rapids, Mich: Zondervan, 1995], p. 90).

Question 5. Help the group to identify with Moses. God was calling him to an awesome task which was far beyond his capabilities. Someone in your group may be in a similar situation.

Question 6. You may want to go ahead and read 3:18, where God explicitly tells Moses they will listen.

Question 10. Don't be satisfied with one simple answer to this question. Have the group explore other possibilities. A poor self-image can lead to different types of sins: false humility which is a form of pride, an avoidance of biblical fellowship, disobedience and so on. Also be sure to take into account the complex factors which cause someone to have a poor self-image, some of which are unrelated to a person's spiritual state.

Question 11. A healthy self-image is not synonymous with self-confidence or self-sufficiency. Our confidence and sufficiency should be in God and his Word. Likewise, Moses' self-image needed to be tempered by a healthy image of God and by his promise "I will be with you."

Study 10. Using Your Spiritual Gifts. 1 Corinthians 12:4-26.

Purpose: To understand the nature and importance of spiritual gifts in order to more effectively serve and build up the body of Christ.

General note. This is a hot issue! There may be someone in your group who insists on the priority of such gifts as tongues, prophecy and healing today. Others may deny their existence altogether, while still others may be completely ignorant of spiritual gifts. A thorough and balanced treatment of spiritual gifts is found in Charles Hummel's *Fire in the Fireplace* (Downers Grove, Ill.: InterVarsity Press, 1993). As you lead the discussion, be sensitive to the different positions within your group. It is essential, however, that you help the group to stick to the passage and understand what this text is actually teaching. Although this is not by any means an exhaustive treatment of spiritual gifts, it provides a necessary foundation for any further consideration of the topic.

This study has questions which deliberately avoid the more controversial aspects of the passage. It focuses instead on those areas which are relevant to all Christians, regardless of their views of spiritual gifts.

Question 1. Some members of your group may be unfamiliar with spiritual gifts. If they ask for a definition at the beginning of the study, tell them that the study itself will help them to understand the nature and purpose of spiritual gifts.

Question 2. According to Margaret E. Thrall: "All forms of *work* and *service* in the Church, resulting from the *varieties of gifts* of the different members, are without exception *the work of one and the same Spirit,* the humbler forms of service no less than the more impressive functions." (*1 and 2 Corinthians* [Cambridge: Cambridge University Press, 1965], p. 87.) In chapter 14 there is a fuller discussion of some of the gifts mentioned here.

Question 3. The gifts are to be used to serve the whole body of Christ. "As the human body must have diversity to work effectively as a whole, so the members of Christ's body have diverse gifts, the use of which can help bring about the accomplishment of Christ's united purpose" (*NIV Study Bible,* p. 1752).

Questions 4—5. Verses 14-20 emphasize that all gifts are important and that there is not a "ranking" of gifts. "Apparently the more spectacular gifts (such as tongues) had been glorified in the Corinthian church, making those who did not have them feel inferior" (*NIV Study Bible,* p. 1752). Verses 21-26 are addressed to those who feel their gifts have a higher value and again emphasize the need for all gifts.

Question 9. Don't let this question turn into an antileadership gripe session. While the Bible affirms the priesthood of all believers, God has clearly placed certain people in positions of responsibility and leadership over his church (Eph 4:11).

Question 10. Some people may be reluctant to share their real feelings, especially if they see themselves as inferior or outsiders in any way. This can be an opportunity to affirm them and build fellowship within your group. Be prepared to spend some time on this.

Study 11. Greatness Through Humility. Mark 10:32-45.

Purpose: To recognize the biblical model of humility and the dangers of pride. To begin renewing our minds and lives in accordance with Jesus' teaching and example.

Question 3. James and John were so concerned about themselves that they failed to hear what Jesus was saying. His words didn't fit all the dreams they hoped would be realized when they reached Jerusalem. They still imagined that Jesus would overthrow the Romans and the corrupt religious leaders and establish his glorious kingdom. When this happened, they expected to be given positions of power, prestige and authority. No wonder their world was turned upside down a few days later!

Question 4. Some group members may feel they don't have a problem with ambition. You might ask them whether they desire recognition, power, prestige or authority.

Question 5. This passage, and especially these verses, takes on added significance when one considers the background of this Gospel. It was written during the reign of the emperor Nero to the Christian community in Rome facing suffering and martyrdom. If time allows, you may want to raise the question of how these words would have been especially relevant for such an audience.

Question 6. The disciples evidently felt that cabinet posts would not be assigned until they reached Jerusalem. They were angry primarily because they thought James and John might have been given the best positions.

Question 8. Help the group to see that Jesus stands the world's concept of greatness on its head. Those who are on the top are really on the bottom, and those who are on the bottom may truly be at the top!

Question 10. Don't let the discussion turn into a gossip session. The goal is to see the prevalence and destructive effects of pride within the Christian community.

Question 12. This question is specific in order to allow people to begin following Christ's example in at least one area. However, as the group discusses this question, people will hear several ideas they can put into practice.

Study 12. Called to Persevere. 2 Timothy 1:8—2:7.

Purpose: To understand the importance of perseverance in the face of suffering and difficulty.

Question 2. It is important to note that Paul is not only calling Timothy to be unashamed of Jesus but also to be unashamed of Paul himself. Why? Because along with Jesus, Paul has been mocked and deserted and is now in prison for his faith. His arrest has made following Christ far less attractive. Nevertheless, Timothy is called to identify unabashedly with Jesus, Paul and the church.

Question 4. Someone may raise the question, "Shouldn't I keep my distance from a Christian who is standing for issues or advocating methods with which I disagree?" You may want to point the group to Jesus' response to the disciples in Luke 9:49-50 where the disciples were faced with a similar temptation.

Question 7. In the face of desertion by others (1:15), Onesiphorous stands out as one who has stood by Paul. "Paul mentions several ways in which this man helped him, and especially he mentions that he was not ashamed of Paul's chains and had actually searched hard for him in Rome. Twice Paul prays mercy for him (16, 18), the second time relating it to *that day,* which must refer to the judgment day of Christ. In view of the reference to Onesiphorus' help at Ephesus, it would seem that he was a consistent helper of the apostle" (*New Bible Commentary,* [Downers Grove, Ill.: InterVarsity Press, 1994], p. 1306).

Question 9. In considering the three metaphors (the soldier, the athlete and farmer) help the group to focus on the nature and requirements of each person's task. Don't let the discussion drift to a debate over such things as the exact nature of the victor's crown (v. 5) or the share of the crops (v. 6). These are not Paul's primary points. Rather he emphasizes that faithful obedience and strenuous labor are necessary for persevering as a disciple of Jesus Christ. For a fuller discussion of the topic see John Stott's *The Message of 2 Timothy* (Downers Grove, Ill.: InterVarsity Press, 1973).

Question 11. You may want to encourage the group to imagine their lives ten or twenty years down the road.

Andrea Sterk is a church historian and an adjunct assistant professor at the University of Notre Dame. Peter Scazzero is the senior pastor of New Life Fellowship Church in Queens, New York. Together they also authored the LifeGuide® Bible Study Christian Disciplines.